Piano Accompaniment

-3

Alfred's

MW00575518

Top Praise & Worship
Instrumental Solos

Arranged by Bill Galliford, Ethan Neuburg and Tod Edmondson

ISBN-10: 0-7390-6601-3
ISBN-13: 978-0-7390-6601-0

CONTENTS

EVERLASTING GOD

Words and Music by
BRENTON BROWN and KEN RILEY

Moderate rock (♩ = 112)

Verse:

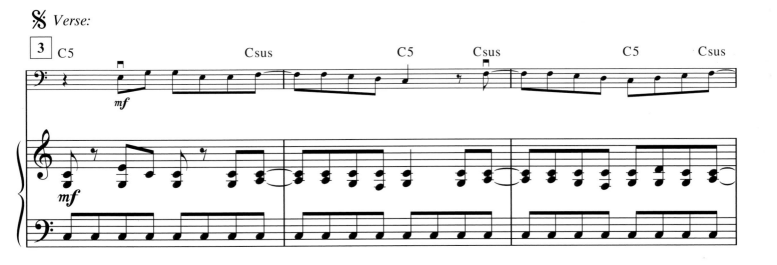

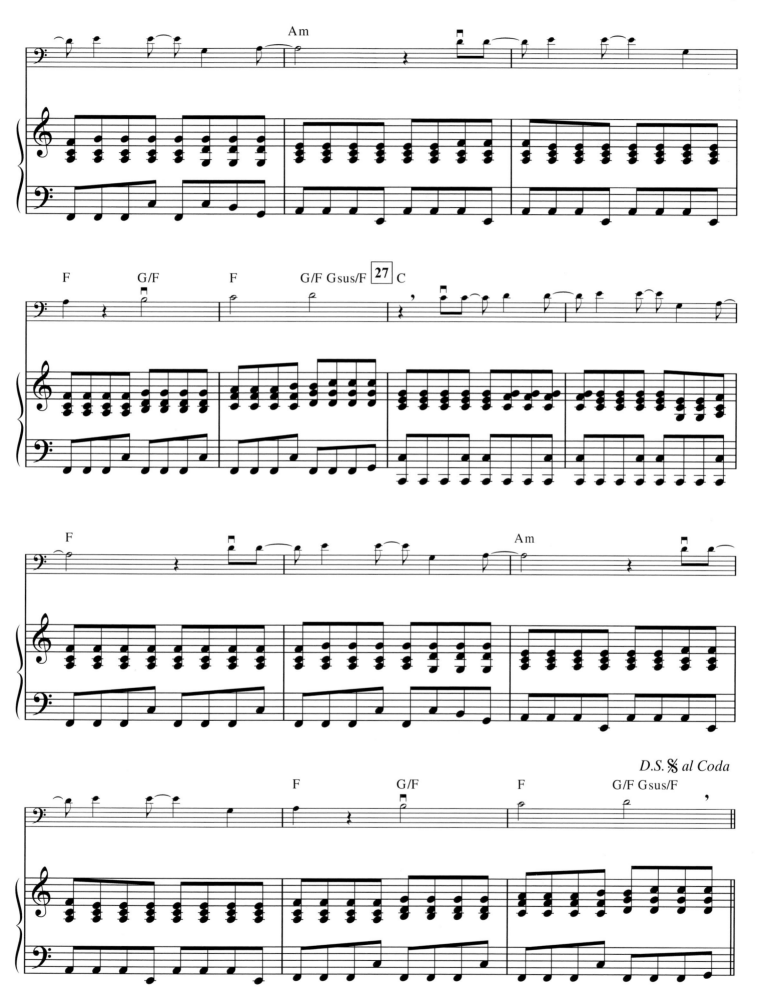

6

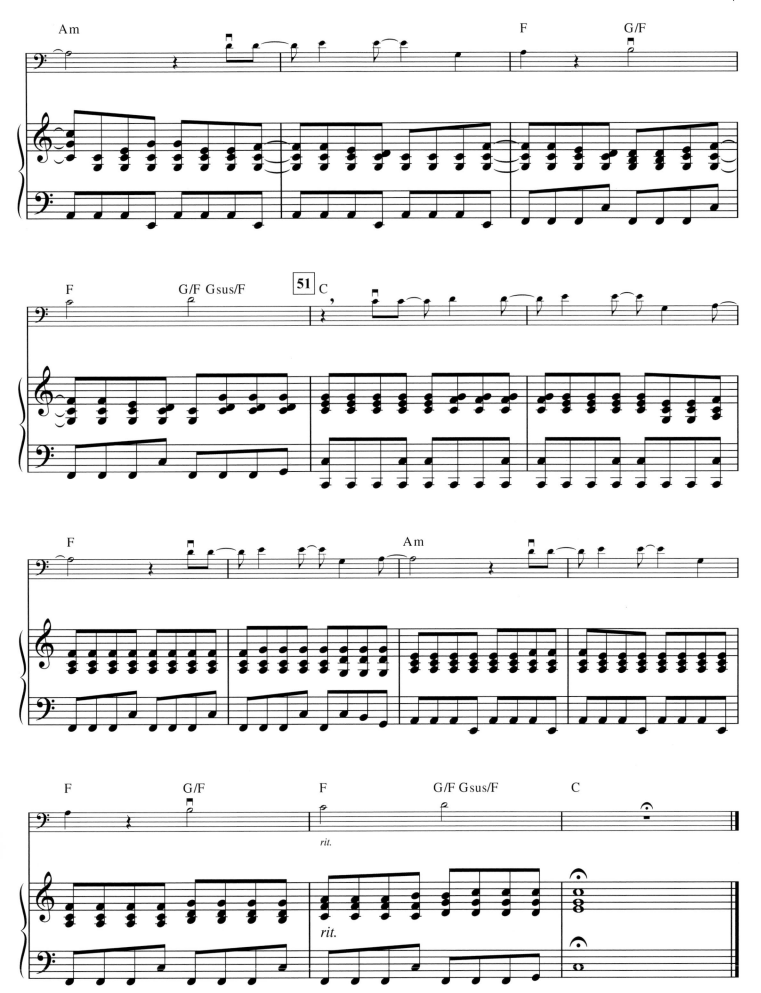

BEAUTIFUL ONE

Words and Music by
TIM HUGHES

Moderate rock (♩ = 120)

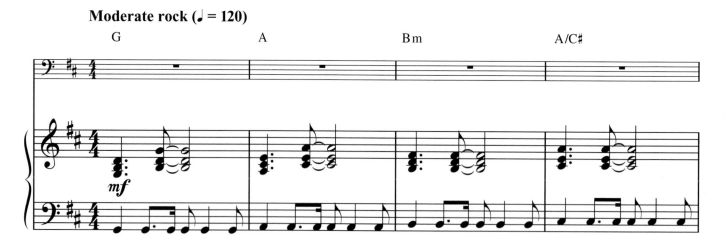

Beautiful One - 4 - 1
34252

10

BLESSED BE YOUR NAME

Words and Music by
BETH REDMAN and MATT REDMAN

Moderate rock (♩ = 120)

Verse:

14

GOD OF WONDERS

Words and Music by
MARC BYRD and STEVE HINDALONG

Moderate rock (♩ = 80)

THE WONDERFUL CROSS

Words and Music by
CHRIS TOMLIN, J.D. WALT
and JESSE REEVES

Moderate rock (♩ = 92)

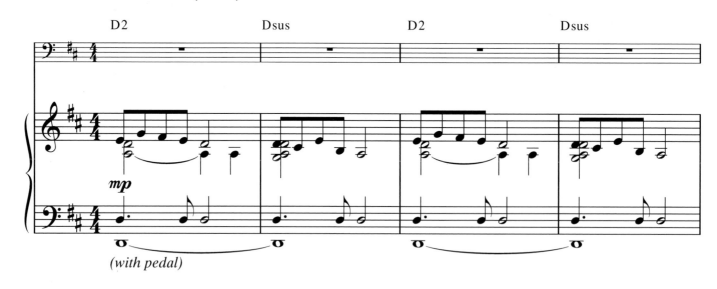

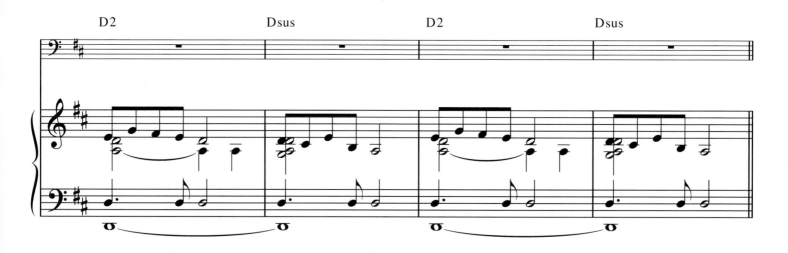

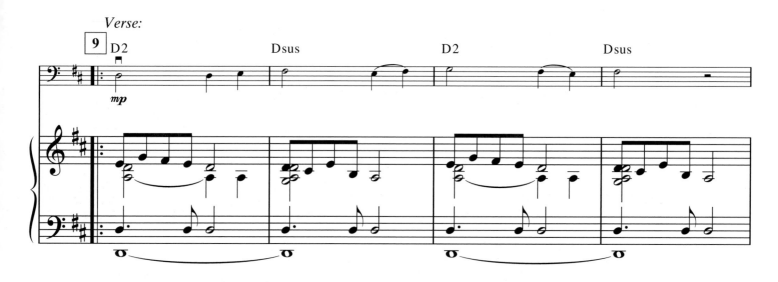

The Wonderful Cross - 4 - 1
34252

The Wonderful Cross - 4 - 4
34252

HERE I AM TO WORSHIP
(LIGHT OF THE WORLD)

Words and Music by
TIM HUGHES

Moderately ($\quarternote$ = 76)

Here I Am to Worship - 3 - 1
34252

26

YOU ARE MY ALL IN ALL

Words and Music by
DENNIS JERNIGAN

Moderately slow (♩ = 72)

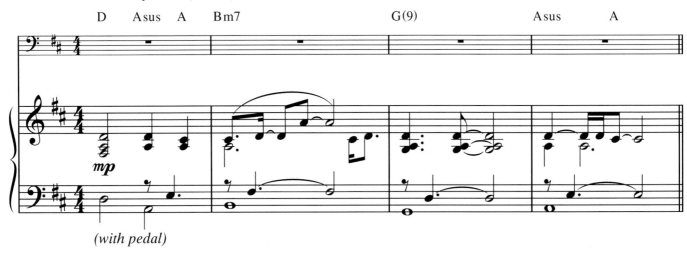

Verse:

You Are My All in All - 3 - 1
34252

28

You Are My All in All - 3 - 2
34252

You Are My All in All - 3 - 3
34252

HOLY IS THE LORD

Words and Music by
CHRIS TOMLIN and LOUIE GIGLIO

32

Holy Is the Lord - 6 - 6
34252

HOW GREAT IS OUR GOD

Words and Music by
CHRIS TOMLIN, ED CASH
and JESSE REEVES

Moderately slow rock (♩ = 76)

Verse 1:

38

Verse 2:

25

Fmaj7

C   Am7

How Great Is Our God - 5 - 3
34252

INDESCRIBABLE

Words and Music by
JESSE REEVES and LAURA STORY

44

Indescribable - 7 - 5
34252

46

JESUS MESSIAH

Words and Music by
**DANIEL CARSON, CHRIS TOMLIN,
ED CASH and JESSE REEVES**

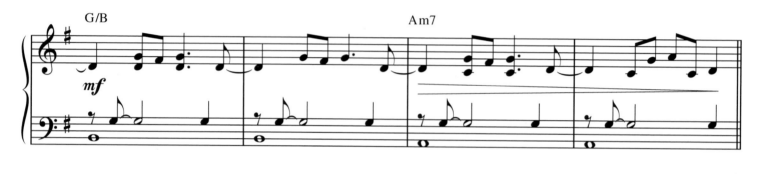

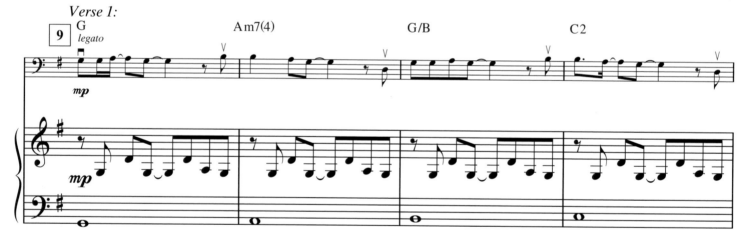

Jesus Messiah - 6 - 1
34252

50

52

Jesus Messiah - 6 - 6
34252

LORD I LIFT YOUR NAME ON HIGH

Words and Music by
RICK FOUNDS

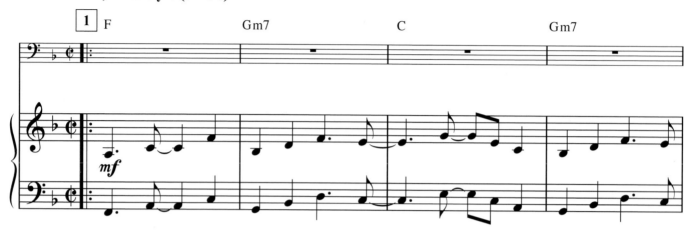

Lord I Lift Your Name on High - 8 - 1
34252

Verse:

56

Chorus:

Lord I Lift Your Name on High - 8 - 3
34252

Lord I Lift Your Name on High - 8 - 4
34252

58

Lord I Lift Your Name on High - 8 - 5
34252

Lord I Lift Your Name on High - 8 - 6
34252

60

Lord I Lift Your Name on High - 8 - 8
34252

MARVELOUS LIGHT

Words and Music by
CHARLIE HALL

Moderate rock (♩ = 126)

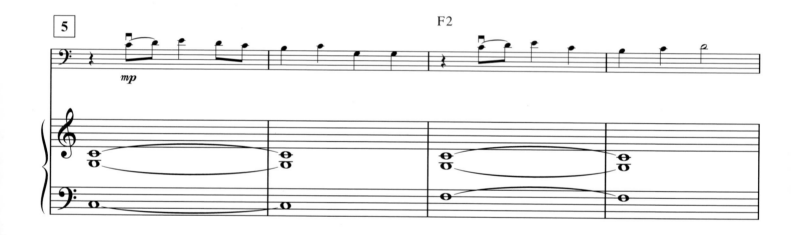

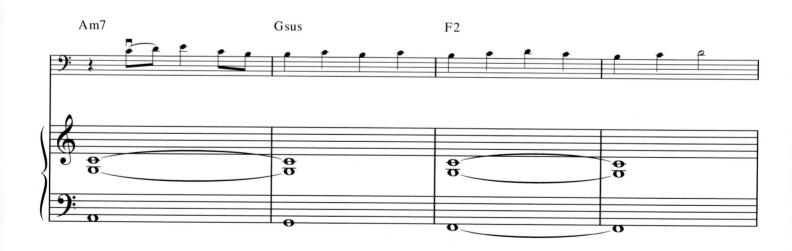

64

Marvelous Light - 6 - 4
34252

66

Marvelous Light - 6 - 6
34252